A GRAPHIC HISTORY OF THE

THE BATTLE OF THE ALAMO

BY GARY JEFFREY
ILLUSTRATED BY NICK SPENDER

Gareth Stevens
Publishing

Please visit our website, www.garethstevens.com.
For a free color catalog of all our high-quality books,
call toll free 1-800-542-2595 or fax 1-877-542-2596.

Library of Congress Cataloging-in-Publication Data

Jeffrey, Gary.
The Battle of the Alamo / Gary Jeffrey.
p. cm. — (A graphic history of the American West)
Includes index.
ISBN 978-1-4339-6729-0 (pbk.)
ISBN 978-1-4339-6730-6 (6-pack)
ISBN 978-1-4339-6727-6 (library binding)
1. Alamo (San Antonio, Tex.)—Siege, 1836—Juvenile literature. I. Title.
F390.J37 2012
976.4'03—dc23
2011022839

First Edition

Published in 2012 by
Gareth Stevens Publishing
111 East 14th Street, Suite 349
New York, NY 10003

Copyright © 2012 David West Books

Designed by David West Books

Photo credits:
p4t, Travis K.Witt

Printed in the United States

CPSIA compliance information: Batch #DW12GS: For further information contact Gareth Stevens, New York, New York at 1-800-542-2595.

CONTENTS

THE FIGHT FOR TEXAS

Mexico gained Texas in 1821, when it won its independence from Spain. The Mexicans encouraged settlement by offering cheap land to Americans. The Texian settlers, as they called themselves, soon outnumbered the local Tejas people. Texians felt it was only a matter of time before their state would become part of the U.S.A.

The Spanish mission San Francisco de los Tejas in San Antonio dates from 1690. Spain named Texas, "Tejas," from a Native American word meaning "friends." Until Mexico took over, hardly anyone had settled in Tejas.

Santa Anna called himself the "Napoleon of the West."

TROUBLED TIMES

In 1834, a Mexican general called Santa Anna took power. Santa Anna wanted to run Mexico as a dictatorship. The Texians rebelled and raised an army. During 1835, they drove the Mexican army out of Texas. Santa Anna vowed to march back in and punish them. Meanwhile, most Texian volunteers thought the war was over and went home.

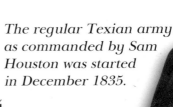

The regular Texian army as commanded by Sam Houston was started in December 1835.

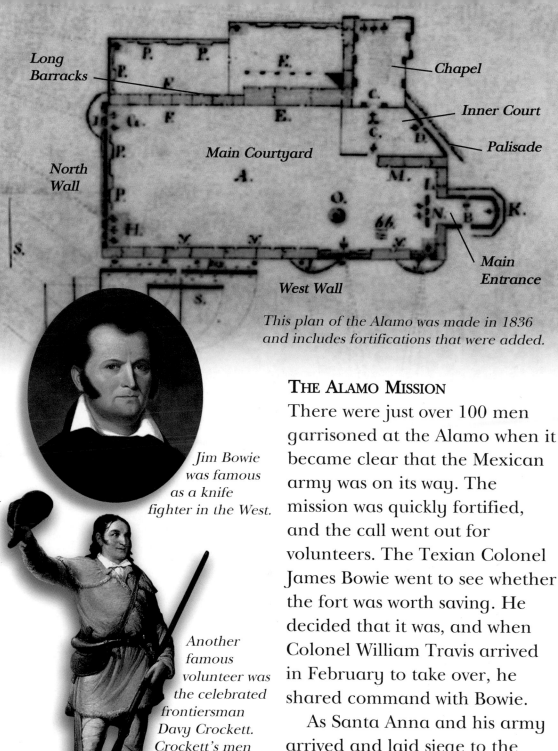

Long
Barracks

Chapel

Inner Court

Palisade

Main Courtyard

North
Wall

Main
Entrance

West Wall

This plan of the Alamo was made in 1836
and includes fortifications that were added.

Jim Bowie
was famous
as a knife
fighter in the West.

Another
famous
volunteer was
the celebrated
frontiersman
Davy Crockett.
Crockett's men
raised the number
of defenders to just
under 200.

THE ALAMO MISSION

There were just over 100 men
garrisoned at the Alamo when it
became clear that the Mexican
army was on its way. The
mission was quickly fortified,
and the call went out for
volunteers. The Texian Colonel
James Bowie went to see whether
the fort was worth saving. He
decided that it was, and when
Colonel William Travis arrived
in February to take over, he
shared command with Bowie.

As Santa Anna and his army
arrived and laid siege to the
fort, Travis begged the Texian
high command to send
reinforcements to help them…

5

THE BATTLE OF THE ALAMO

MARCH 3, 1836. DAVY CROCKETT AND COLONEL TRAVIS WATCHED FROM THE ALAMO'S RAMPARTS AS 1,000 MEXICAN SOLDIERS MARCHED INTO SANTA ANNA'S CAMP IN SAN ANTONIO.

THERE'S GOT TO BE MORE THAN TWO THOUSAND OF THEM NOW, ALTOGETHER.

HOW MUCH LONGER DO YOU THINK THESE WALLS CAN HOLD OUT?

MARCH 4. IN BEXAR, SANTA ANNA LISTENED TO HIS GENERALS AT A COUNCIL OF WAR.

SIR, MOST OF US AGREE THAT WE SHOULD WAIT FOR THE HEAVY GUNS TO ARRIVE BEFORE WE...

NO, NO, NO! THIS LITTLE FORT HAS HELD US UP FOR TOO LONG.

BUT IT WILL COST US MANY MEN.

SOLDIERS' LIVES ARE WORTH NO MORE THAN *CHICKENS!*

8

THE ALAMO *MUST* FALL. COST WHAT IT *MAY*.

HE ORDERED THE ATTACK TO BEGIN ON MARCH 6. BY THEN, THERE WOULD BE MORE THAN 5,000 MEN SURROUNDING THE FORT.

MARCH 6, 4:00 A.M. A MASS OF MEXICAN SOLDIERS ADVANCED ON ALL FOUR WALLS OF THE FORT.

FOR MEXICO!

FOR SANTA ANNA! AAGH!

ONLY TO BE DRIVEN BACK *TWICE*.

THE MEXICAN COMMANDERS ORDERED THEIR TROOPS FORWARD AGAIN. THIS TIME, THEY MANAGED TO SCALE THE WALLS AND REACH THE RAMPARTS OF THE FORT.

IT WAS A DESPERATE FIGHT. THE DEFENDERS WERE DETERMINED TO CLAIM AS MANY ENEMY LIVES AS POSSIBLE.

DEFENDING THE NORTH WALL, TRAVIS TOOK A SHOT TO THE HEAD AND WAS KILLED INSTANTLY.

CRACK!

ARRGH!

AS PLATOONS OF MEXICANS STREAMED INTO THE COMPOUND, THE DEFENDERS WHEELED A CANNON AROUND INTO THE COURTYARD.

VICTORY OR DEATH!

BOOM!

AIEEEEEEEE!

THEY GOT OFF JUST TWO SHOTS BEFORE THEY WERE ALL KILLED.

SOME OF THE TEXIANS HAD LOCKED THEMSELVES IN THE BARRACKS. FROM THEIR RIFLE HOLES, THEY SHOT AS MANY OF THE ENEMY AS THEY COULD.

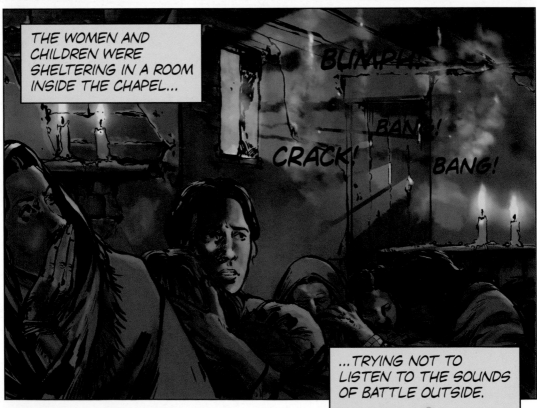

THE WOMEN AND CHILDREN WERE SHELTERING IN A ROOM INSIDE THE CHAPEL...

BUMPH!

BANG!

CRACK!

BANG!

...TRYING NOT TO LISTEN TO THE SOUNDS OF BATTLE OUTSIDE.

DEADLY SICK WITH FEVER, JIM BOWIE LAY IN HIS COT IN THE CHAPEL'S OLD BAPTISTRY. HIS FAMOUS HUNTING KNIFE WAS AT HIS SIDE.

EITHER WAY, LORD, I'M *READY...*

THE MEXICANS AIMED THE CAPTURED GUN AT THE LONG BARRACKS DOOR AND...

CRASH!

CROCKETT AND HIS MEN WERE MAKING A LAST STAND BEHIND A LOW WALL IN FRONT OF THE CHAPEL. BUT THEY WERE TERRIBLY EXPOSED.

THEY'VE GOT A GUN ON US!

GET DOWN!

BOOOM!

SANTA ANNA'S MEN SWARMED ONTO THE INNER COURT.

THE SOLDIERS BURST IN ON THE WOMEN AND CHILDREN. A WOUNDED YOUNG FIGHTER, CAUGHT TRYING TO HIDE, WAS KILLED RIGHT IN FRONT OF SUSANNA DICKINSON.

NO!

BY 8:00 A.M. IT WAS OVER. SANTA ANNA CAME TO LOOK AT THE BATTLEFIELD.

THERE ARE THE CHICKENS. MUCH BLOOD HAS BEEN SHED.

19

MEANWHILE, GENERAL CASTRILLON HAD DISCOVERED FIVE TEXIANS HIDING UNDER A MATTRESS IN THE LONG BARRACKS.

I SAID **NO** PRISONERS!

BUT SIR, THESE MEN ARE THE ONLY ONES-

SANTA ANNA TURNED HIS BACK WHILE HIS OFFICERS CHARGED IN WITH THEIR SWORDS.

REMEMBER THE ALAMO!

When Sam Houston learned of the Alamo's defeat, he ordered a retreat to the US border, burning towns as he went. The only things holding the Mexican army back were impassable rivers swollen by rains. Houston used a precious two-week respite to train the many new volunteers who had rallied to the cause.

Santa Anna's ruthless tactics included the execution of more than 300 Texian prisoners captured at Goliad.

TURNING POINT

Santa Anna was determined to end the war quickly. He divided his army and raced to capture the Texas leadership at Galveston. At the same time, Houston turned around and faced him, meeting at San Jacinto. Houston told his soldiers to remember the Alamo and Goliad. The Texians won a stunning victory

Victory at San Jacinto enabled Texas to become a republic. The adding of Texas to the U.S.A. in 1846 caused a major war with Mexico. After the Mexicans were defeated, the U.S.A. gained what would become New Mexico, Arizona, Nevada, California, and Utah—roughly a third of modern America.